GREEN PLANET
RECYCLING

by Rebecca Pettiford

pogo

Ideas for Parents and Teachers

Pogo Books let children practice reading informational text while introducing them to nonfiction features such as headings, labels, sidebars, maps, and diagrams, as well as a table of contents, glossary, and index.

Carefully leveled text with a strong photo match offers early fluent readers the support they need to succeed.

Before Reading

- "Walk" through the book and point out the various nonfiction features. Ask the student what purpose each feature serves.

- Look at the glossary together. Read and discuss the words.

Read the Book

- Have the child read the book independently.

- Invite him or her to list questions that arise from reading.

After Reading

- Discuss the child's questions. Talk about how he or she might find answers to those questions.

- Prompt the child to think more. Ask: What sorts of things do you recycle at your house? How about at school?

Pogo Books are published by Jump!
5357 Penn Avenue South
Minneapolis, MN 55419
www.jumplibrary.com

Library of Congress Cataloging-in-Publication Data

Names: Pettiford, Rebecca, author.
Title: Recycling / by Rebecca Pettiford.
Description: Minneapolis, MN: Jump!, Inc. [2016] | Series: Green planet | Audience: Ages 7-10.
Includes bibliographical references and index.
Identifiers: LCCN 2016015834 (print)
LCCN 2016016184 (ebook)
ISBN 9781620314036 (hardcover: alk. paper)
ISBN 9781624964503 (ebook)
Subjects: LCSH: Recycling (Waste, etc.)–Juvenile literature.
Salvage (Waste, etc.)–Juvenile literature.
Classification: LCC TD794.5 .P49 2016 (print)
LCC TD794.5 (ebook) | DDC 363.72/82–dc23
LC record available at https://lccn.loc.gov/2016015834

Series Editor: Jenny Fretland VanVoorst
Series Designer: Anna Peterson
Book Designer: Leah Sanders
Photo Researchers: Kirsten Chang and Leah Sanders

Photo Credits: All photos by Shutterstock except: Getty, 5, 10-11, 12-13, 14-15, 19; iStock, 8, 16-17; Superstock, 20-21; Thinkstock, 1, 3.

Printed in the United States of America at Corporate Graphics in North Mankato, Minnesota.

TABLE OF CONTENTS

CHAPTER 1

WHY DO WE RECYCLE?

People throw out tons of waste. In the United States alone, 220 million tons (200 million metric tons) of waste are created every year. Where does it all go?

It goes into **landfills**. Some of it is burned. Some of it even ends up in the ocean! How can we make less waste? We can **recycle** many goods. We can make new things from glass, metal, paper, and plastic.

Recycling helps the **environment**. We do not need to use as many **resources** to make new goods. This helps save the forests and rivers where animals live.

When we burn less waste, the air is cleaner. Putting less waste in landfills helps keep the **groundwater** cleaner.

CHAPTER 2

RECYCLING IN ACTION

You may have recycling bins at home or school. One is for paper. One is for glass. Another is for plastic.

What happens when the bins are emptied into a truck? Let's find out.

Trucks go to a **recycling plant**. Workers unload them. They put the goods on a **conveyor**. They sort the goods by type. They clean them. Soon, the goods are ready to be recycled.

DID YOU KNOW?

Recycling creates jobs. As more people recycle, the number of workers needed to gather and prepare the goods grows.

Different things are recycled in different ways. Glass is crushed. It is heated, melted, and put into **casts**. It is shaped into new bottles and jars.

Metal is also heated and melted. It is put into casts. It can be turned into new cans or even new cars!

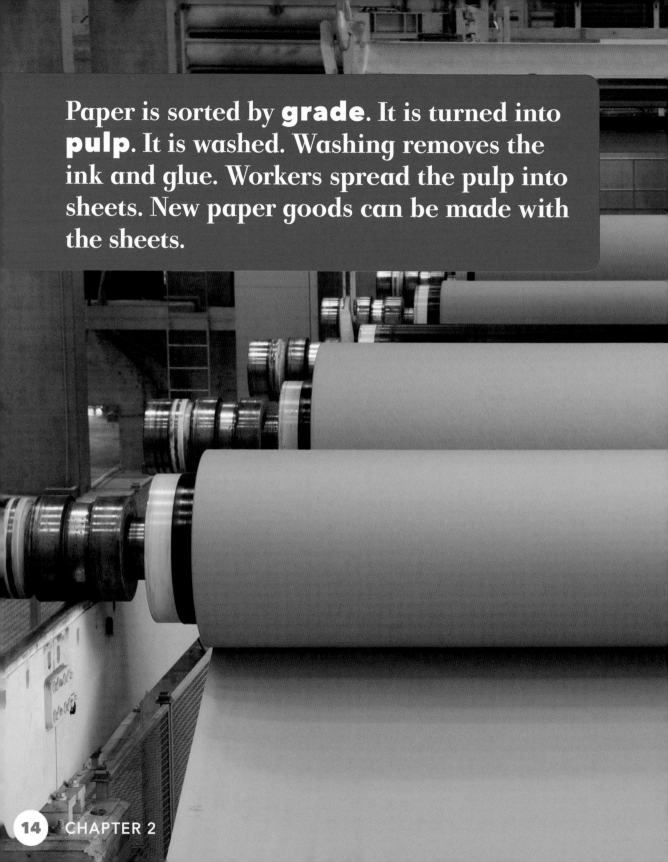

Paper is sorted by **grade**. It is turned into **pulp**. It is washed. Washing removes the ink and glue. Workers spread the pulp into sheets. New paper goods can be made with the sheets.

How does old paper turn into new paper?
Let's take a closer look.

① Paper is sorted.

③ Pulp is washed and dried.

② Paper is turned in pulp.

④ Pulp is formed into sheets.

Plastic is ground into flakes. The flakes are washed and dried. Then they are melted and formed into beads. The beads are used to make carpeting and floor mats. Some plastic is made into fake wood. This saves trees.

plastic flakes

CHAPTER 3

OTHER WAYS TO RECYCLE

A lot of food and garden waste ends up in landfills. It breaks down and gives off a harmful gas called **methane**.

You can turn food and garden waste into **compost**. It will make your soil and plants healthy.

reusable bag ·····▶

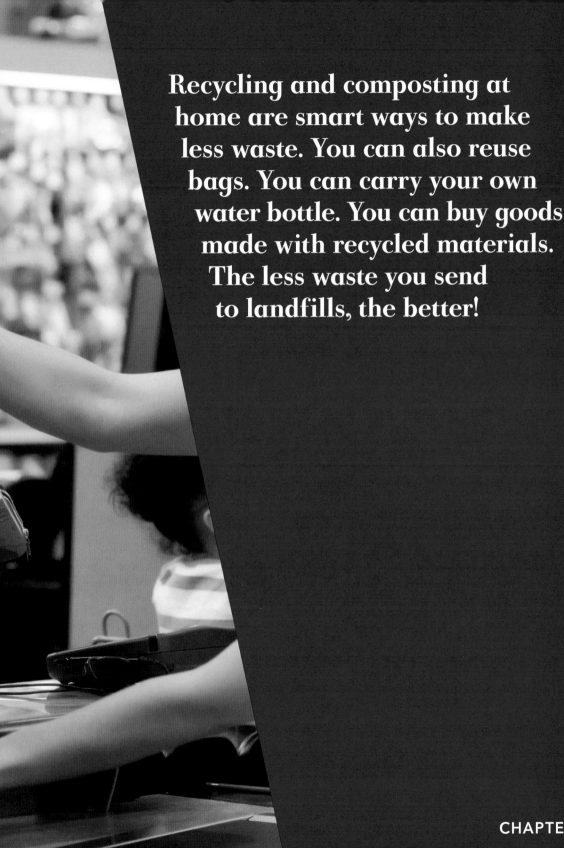

Recycling and composting at home are smart ways to make less waste. You can also reuse bags. You can carry your own water bottle. You can buy goods made with recycled materials. The less waste you send to landfills, the better!

ACTIVITIES & TOOLS

MAKE YOUR OWN COMPOST

1. Get a compost bin. You can make or buy one with an adult's help. The bin should have good drainage. This lets extra water out. You will layer green and brown waste in it.

2. Start with a brown layer (dry leaves, twigs, paper, and coffee filters).

3. Then add a green layer (green grass clippings, leaves, vegetables, fruit, egg shells, and coffee grounds). Do not add meat, bones, or dairy foods.

4. Add another brown layer. Alternate the green and brown layers in the pile.

5. Add water. Make sure the pile is moist but not too wet.

6. Mix the layers regularly so air mixes in. The air will help the waste break down faster.

7. The bin will get hot. Your compost is cooking! Keep mixing. When it looks like dark crumbs, it is ready for your garden.

GLOSSARY

casts: Forms into which liquid metal, glass, or plastic is poured in order to create a new item.

compost: A mixture of matter that used to be alive (such as grass) or its products (such as paper) that is used to improve soil.

conveyor: A machine that moves things from place to place.

environment: The surroundings or conditions in which a person, animal, or plant lives.

grade: The classification given to paper based on different characteristics.

groundwater: Underground water that supplies wells and springs.

landfills: Places to bury waste beneath layers of earth.

methane: A greenhouse gas that warms the planet's surface and is harmful to the environment.

pulp: A soft, wet mass of material made from paper or wood.

recycle: To make something new from something that has already been used.

recycling plant: A place where items like paper, glass, and plastic are prepared for recycling.

resources: In nature, things such as minerals, water, and land that can be used to make goods for sale.

INDEX

TO LEARN MORE

Learning more is as easy as 1, 2, 3.

1) Go to www.factsurfer.com

2) Enter "recycling" into the search box.

3) Click the "Surf" button to see a list of websites.

With factsurfer, finding more information is just a click away.